Coco Chanel

Quotes & Facts

By Blago Kirov

First Edition

*****

Coco Chanel: Quotes & Facts
*****

Copyright © 2015 by Blago Kirov

Foreword

"A girl should be two things: classy and fabulous."

This book is an anthology of Quotes from Coco Chanel and Facts about Coco Chanel. It grants her reflections on subjects ranging from Women and Men to Elegance and Fashion; in addition, the book shows the personality of Coco Chanel into a different light:

While working as a cafe and concert singer, Chanel adopted the name, Coco. Coco's real first name is Gabrielle; she got Coco from a song she performed in a musical called 'Qui qu'a vu Coco'.
While Coco was living with Etienne Balsan, a playboy and polo player, she began to design hats as a hobby.
The Chanel No.5 scent is the best selling in the world.
Coco Chanel had never been married.
For over 30 years, Chanel considered Ritz, one of the most luxurious hotels in Paris, her home.
Coco Chanel was a very superstitious person; she surrounded herself with talismans and lucky charms.
Coco Chanel died in 1971 at the Ritz Hotel in Paris at the age of 88.
Coco Chanel created looks for Gloria Swanson for the film "Tonight or Never", while Greta Garbo and Marlene Dietrich became her private clients.

"I never wanted to weigh more heavily on a man than a bird."
"A girl should be two things: classy and fabulous."
"Elegance is refusal."
"A woman who doesn't wear perfume has no future."
"A woman with good shoes is never ugly!"

"Elegance comes from being as beautiful inside as outside."
"Fashion fades, only style remains the same."
"A woman has the age she deserves."
"I don't do fashion, I AM fashion."

Some Facts about Coco Chanel

While working as a cafe and concert singer, Chanel adopted the name, Coco. Coco's real first name is Gabrielle; she got Coco from a song she performed in a musical called 'Qui qu'a vu Coco'.

While Coco was living with Etienne Balsan, a playboy and polo player, she began to design hats as a hobby.

The Chanel No.5 scent is the best selling in the world.

Coco Chanel had never been married.

For over 30 years, Chanel considered Ritz, one of the most luxurious hotels in Paris, her home.

Coco Chanel was a very superstitious person; she surrounded herself with talismans and lucky charms.

Coco Chanel died in 1971 at the Ritz Hotel in Paris at the age of 88.

Coco Chanel created looks for Gloria Swanson for the film Tonight or Never, while Greta Garbo and Marlene Dietrich became her private clients.

Coco Chanel was born August 19th, 1883 in Saumur, a small city in France.

Coco Chanel had two sisters, Julie and Antoinette and three brothers, Alphonse, Lucien and Augustine.

When Coco Chanel was just twelve years old her mother died, leaving her father to care for the six children.

For seven years, Coco was in the orphanage of the Catholic monastery of Aubazine. At the age of eighteen, she left the orphanage and began work for a local tailor.

While Coco was living with Etienne Balsan, a playboy and polo player, she began to design hats as a hobby.

In 1909, with the help of Etienne Balsan and Arthur Edward "Boy" Capel, another rich lover, Coco Chanel was able to open in Paris her own millinery, or hat shop called "Chanel Modes."

In 1913 at her new boutique in Deauville, France, Coco introduced her sportswear for women.

Coco Chanel became romantically involved with Hans Gunther von Dincklage, a German officer 13 years her junior, who was in the German military intelligence service.

Coco Chanel made the tan popular after retuning from a cruise to Cannes with sunburn.

In 1925 Coco Chanel introduced her signature cardigan jacket.

In 1926 Coco Chanel brought out the little black dress and not only made it very popular, but also versatile; it could be worn day or night. She recounted that her legendary 'little black dress' originated in 1920 when she went to the Opera and observed many women wearing all different colored dresses that she was not a fan of. Her ideology was that dressing in black symbolized power and liberty.

Coco Chanel also introduces the bobbed hair style, pants for women, skiing accessories, she eliminated the use of the corset from women's fashion, added the use of knit jersey and unveiled the women's bathing suit.

Chanel No. 5 got its name because the number five was Coco Chanel's lucky number.

Coco Chanel never fully owned the House of Chanel or its many products. Pierre Wertheimer, her partner retained the majority of the profits, giving her a 10%.

Coco Chanel was a Leo and collected anything with lions.

Coco Channel loved pockets, and believed there are not enough of them in women's clothes.

Coco was one of the first to employ the celebrities to promote her inventions. She photographed famous actresses wearing the clothes she designed for the advertising.

Coco Chanel also was a Hollywood fashion director. To attract women to the theater, Coco was asked to design costumes that would appeal to the women.

In 1938 Coco decided to retire and for the next fifteen years she moved back and forth between Vichy and Switzerland.

In 1954, she decided to make a come back and introduced the pea jacket and bell bottom pants for women.

Katharine Hepburn, played Coco in a Broadway musical, "Coco" based on Coco Chanel's life.

Coco Chanel introduced her first perfume, Chanel No. 5, in 1922, and it was one of the first perfumes ever to mix natural and artificial essences.

The shape of her Chanel No.5 bottle was inspired from Place Vendome.

Until her death in 1971, her fashion empire brought in more than $160 million per year.

Before her designing career began, Coco Chanel worked in a small hosiery shop in France.

Coco Chanel became a licensed hat-maker and owned her first shop in 1910.

Coco Chanel invented the "Little Black Dress" in 1926, which French Vogue dubbed "Chanel's Ford", for its practicality and marketability.

Coco Chanel is credited with popularizing the concept of "costume jewelry" in the 1920s, creating seasonal jewelry that mixed fake pearls with real stones.

Coco Chanel introduced the idea of using jersey fabric to create clothing, which had prior been used only for men's undergarments.

Coco Chanel and her brand are most well known for costume jewelry, two-tone shoes, quilted bags, and simple suits made of tweed or jersey.

A bottle of the classic Chanel No. 5 is sold every 30 seconds.

Coco Chanel had Chanel No. 5 sprayed throughout her home.

Coco Chanel introduced the iconic quilted 2.55 classic flap bag in February 1955, hence the name 2.55.

Her classic Chanel suit became famous for its flattering cut, simple fabric, and specially weighted lining, to give it that perfect hang.

Coco Chanel was named as one of the 100 most influential people of the 20th century.

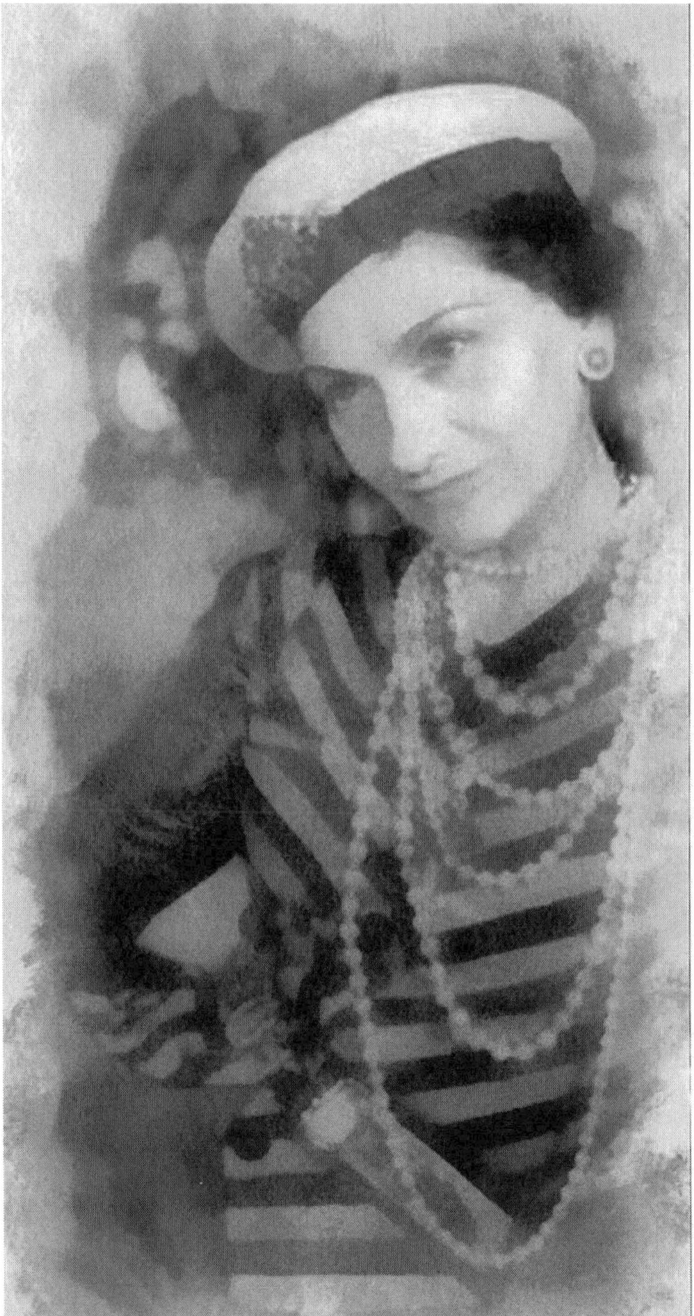

The double C of the Chanel logo is an abbreviation of Chanel and Capel. Arthur Capel was one of Chanel's lovers, and he helped her set up the House of Chanel.

Chanel No. 5 didn't become so famous until Marilyn Monroe gave the most fascinating answer for LIFE magazine. "What do you wear to bed?" the magazine asked her. "Just a few drops of Chanel No. 5," she responded.

Some of her famous American clientele included Elizabeth Taylor, Jane Fonda, Jackie Kennedy, and Grace Kelly.

Her Words

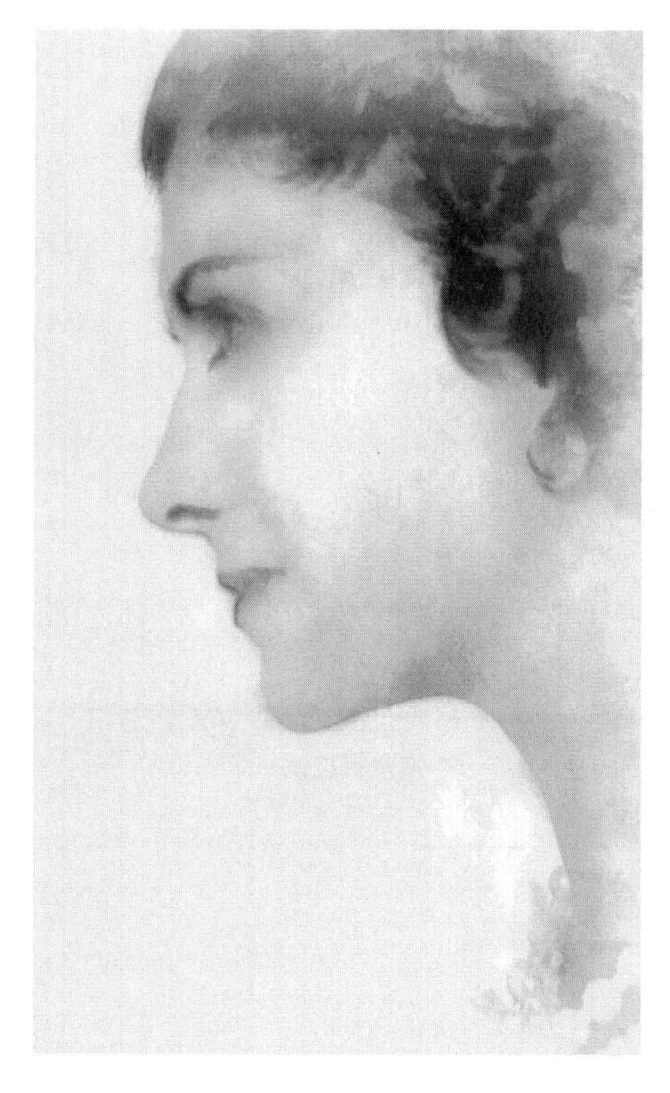

"I don't do fashion, I AM fashion."

"A beautiful dress may look beautiful on a hanger, but that means nothing. It must be seen on the shoulders, with the movement of the arms, the legs, and the waist."

"A fashion that does not reach the streets is not a fashion"

"A girl should be two things: classy and fabulous."

"A girl should be two things: who and what she wants."

"A style does not go out of style as long as it adapts itself to its period. When there is an incompatibility between the style and a certain state of mind, it is never the style that triumphs."

"A woman has the age she deserves."

"A woman should wear perfume wherever she wants to be kissed."

"A woman who cuts her hair is about to change her life."

"A woman who doesn't wear perfume has no future."

"A woman with good shoes i never ugly!"

"A woman's education consists of two lessons: never leave the house without stocking, never go out without a hat."

"Adornment is never anything except a reflection of the heart."

"Adornment, what a science! Beauty, what a weapon! Modesty, what elegance!"

"Arrogance is in everything I do. It is in my gestures, the harshness of my voice, in the glow of my gaze, in my sinewy, tormented face."

"As long as you know men are like children, you know everything!"

"As long as you know that most men are like children, you know everything."

"As soon as you set foot on a yacht you belong to some man, not to yourself, and you die of boredom."

"Ask me who I don't dress!"

"Be classy. Anything but trashy."

"Capel said, "Remember that you're a woman." All too often I forgot that."

"Clothes by a man who doesn't know women, never had one, and dreams of being one!"

"Coquetry, it's a triumph of the spirit over the senses."

"Costume jewelry is not made to give women an aura of wealth,

"Don't spend time beating on a wall, hoping to transform it into a door."

"Dress shabbily, they notice the dress. Dress impeccably, they notice the woman."

"Elegance comes from being as beautiful inside as outside."

"Elegance does not consist in putting on a new dress."

"Elegance is not the prerogative of those who have just escaped from adolescence, but of those who have already taken possession of their future."

"Elegance is refusal."

"Everyone marries the Duke of Westminster. There are a lot of duchesses, but only one Coco Chanel."

"Fashion fades, only style remains the same."

"Fashion has two purposes: comfort and love. Beauty comes when fashion succeeds."

"Fashion is always of the time in which you live. It is not something standing alone. But the grand problem, the most important problem, is to rejuvenate women. To make women look young. Then their outlook changes. They feel more joyous."

"Fashion is architecture: it is a matter of proportions."

"Fashion is made to become unfashionable."

"Fashion is not something that exists in dresses only. Fashion is in the sky, in the street, fashion has to do with ideas, the way we live, what is happening."

"For a woman betrayal has no sense - one cannot betray one's passions."

"Gentleness doesn't get work done unless you happen to be a hen laying eggs."

"Great loves too must be endured."

"Guilt is perhaps the most painful companion of death."

"Hard times arouse an instinctive desire for authenticity."

"He will soon be claiming that the Resistance has liberated the world"

"How many cares one loses when one decides not to be something but to be someone."

"I am not young but I feel young. The day I feel old, I will go to bed and stay there. J'aime la vie! I feel that to live is a wonderful thing."

"I don't know why women want any of the things men have when one of the things that women have is men."

"I don't care what you think about me. I don't think about you at all."

"I don't do fashion, I AM fashion."

"I don't know why women want any of the things men have when one the things that women have is men."

"I don't understand how a woman can leave the house without fixing herself up a little - if only out of politeness. And then, you never know, maybe that's the day she has a date with destiny. And it's best to be as pretty as possible for destiny."

"I imposed black; it still going strong today, for black wipes out everything else around"

"I invented my life by taking for granted that everything I did not like would have an opposite, which I would like."

"I love luxury. And luxury lies not in richness and ornaments but in the absence of vulgarity. Vulgarity is the ugliest word in our language. I stay in the game to fight it."

"I never wanted to weigh more heavily on a man than a bird."

"I wanted to give a woman comfortable clothes that would flow with her body. A woman is closest to being naked when she is well-dressed."

"If a man talks bad about all women, it usually means he was burned by one woman."

"If you were born without wings, do nothing to prevent them from growing."

"In 1919 I woke up famous. I'd never guessed it. If I'd known I was famous, I'd have stolen away and wept. I was stupid. I was supposed to be intelligent. I was sensitive and very dumb."

"In order to be irreplaceable one must be unique"

"Innovation! One cannot be forever innovating. I want to create classics."

"It is always better to be slightly underdressed."

"It's probably not just by chance that I'm alone. It would be very hard for a man to live with me, unless he's terribly strong. And if he's stronger than I, I'm the one who can't live with him. ... I'm neither smart nor stupid, but I don't think I'm a run-of-the-mill person. I've been in business without being a business-woman, I've loved without being a woman made only for love. The two men I've loved, I think, will remember me, on earth or in heaven, because men always remember a woman who caused them concern and uneasiness. I've done my best, in regard to people and to life, without precepts, but with a taste for justice."

"Jump out the window if you are the object of passion. Flee it if you feel it. Passion goes, boredom remains."

"Look for the woman in the dress. If there is no woman, there is no dress."

"Luxury lies not in the richness of things, but in the absence of vulgarity"

"Luxury must be comfortable, otherwise it is not luxury."

"Material things aside, we need no advice but approval."

"My friends, there are no friends."

"My life didn't please me, so I created my life."

"Nature gives you the face you have at twenty. Life shapes the face you have at thirty. But at fifty you get the face you deserve."

"Nothing goes out of fashion sooner than a long dress with a very low neck."

"Nothing is ugly as long as it is alive."

"Only those with no memory insist on their originality."

"Passion goes, Boredom remains."

"Simplicity is the keynote of all true elegance."

"Sin can be forgiven, but stupid is forever."

"Since everything is in our heads, we had better not lose them."

"Some people think luxury is the opposite of poverty. It is not. It is the opposite of vulgarity."

"Success is most often achieved by those who don't know that failure is inevitable."

"The best color in the whole world, is the one that looks good, on you!"

"The best things in life are free. The second best things are very, very expensive."

"The most courageous act is still to think for yourself. Aloud."

"There are people who have money and people who are rich."

"There have been several Duchesses of Westminster but there is only one Chanel!"

"There is a time for work, and a time for love. That leaves no other time."

"There is no time for cut-and-dried monotony. There is time for work. And time for love. That leaves no other time!"

"There is nothing more comfortable than a caterpillar and nothing more made for love than a butterfly. We need dresses that crawl and dresses that fly. Fashion is at once a caterpillar and a butterfly, caterpillar by day, butterfly by night"

"There is nothing worse than solitude. Solitude can help a man realize himself; but it destroys a woman"

"Those who create are rare; those who cannot are numerous. Therefore, the latter are stronger."

"When I can no longer create anything, I'll be done for."

"Where perfume should be worn: wherever one wants to be kissed."

"Why am I so determined to put the shoulder where it belongs? Women have very round shoulders that push forward slightly; this touches me and I say: One must not hide that! Then someone tells you: The shoulder is on the back. I've never seen women with shoulders on their backs."

"Women have always been the strong ones of the world. The men are always seeking from women a little pillow to put their heads down on. They are always longing for the mother who held them as infants."

"Women must tell men always that they are the strong ones. They are the big, the strong, the wonderful. In truth, women are the strong ones. It is just my opinion, I am not a professor."

"Women think of all colors except the absence of color. I have said that black has it all. White too. Their beauty is absolute. It is the perfect harmony."

"You can be gorgeous at thirty, charming at forty, and irresistible for the rest of your life."

"You live but once; you might as well be amusing."

"Youth is something very new: Twenty years ago no one mentioned it."

Printed in Great Britain
by Amazon